D1165104

WORKING WITH FRACTIONS

by
David A. Adler

illustrated by
Edward Miller

Holiday House
New York

4
2
1
6
5
7

A **fraction** is a **part** of something.

You can see fractions at birthday parties.

If there are 3 red balloons at the party and 10 balloons in all,

then a part, a fraction, of the balloons is red.

$\frac{3}{10}$ of the balloons are red.

If you play musical chairs at the party and 5 of the 7 children are sitting on chairs, a fraction of the children is sitting.

$\frac{5}{7}$ of the children are sitting on chairs.

If a pizza pie is served at the party and the pie is cut into 8 equal slices, then each slice is a part, a fraction, of the pie. Each slice is $\frac{1}{8}$ of the pie.

If the birthday cake is cut into 12 equal slices, then each slice is a part, a fraction, of the cake. Each slice is $\frac{1}{12}$ of the cake.

Fractions are not only found at birthday parties.

Fractions are also found everywhere.

Think of how you use fractions every day.

Each time you read a page in a book,

you are reading just a part, a fraction,

of the book. If the book is 96 pages,

each page is $\frac{1}{96}$ of the book.

Coins are fractions too. There are 20 nickels

in a dollar. Each nickel is a part, a fraction,

of a dollar. Each nickel is 1 of 20 nickels in

a dollar. Each nickel is $\frac{1}{20}$ of a dollar.

$$\frac{1}{20}$$

Now you know some fractions.

You know $\frac{3}{10}$, $\frac{5}{7}$, $\frac{1}{8}$, $\frac{1}{12}$, $\frac{1}{96}$, and $\frac{1}{20}$.

Take a look at $\frac{3}{10}$, the fraction of balloons that are red. The 3 tells you we are talking about 3 red balloons. The 10 tells you that there are 10 balloons in all.

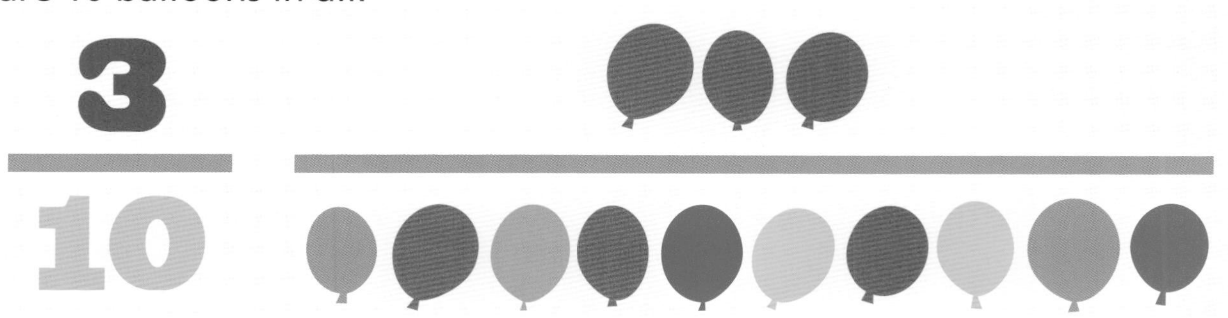

Take a look at $\frac{5}{7}$, the musical chairs fraction. The 5 tells you we are talking about 5 children, the 5 who are sitting. The 7 tells you that there are 7 children in all.

Take a look at $\frac{1}{8}$, the pizza slice fraction. The 1 tells you we are talking about 1 slice of pizza. The 8 tells you we are talking about 8 slices in all.

Each fraction has a top number and a bottom number. The top number of a fraction is the **numerator**. The bottom number is the **denominator**.

In the fraction $\frac{3}{10}$, the numerator is 3. The denominator is 10.

In the fraction $\frac{5}{7}$, the numerator is 5. The denominator is 7.

In the fraction $\frac{1}{8}$, the numerator is 1. The denominator is 8.

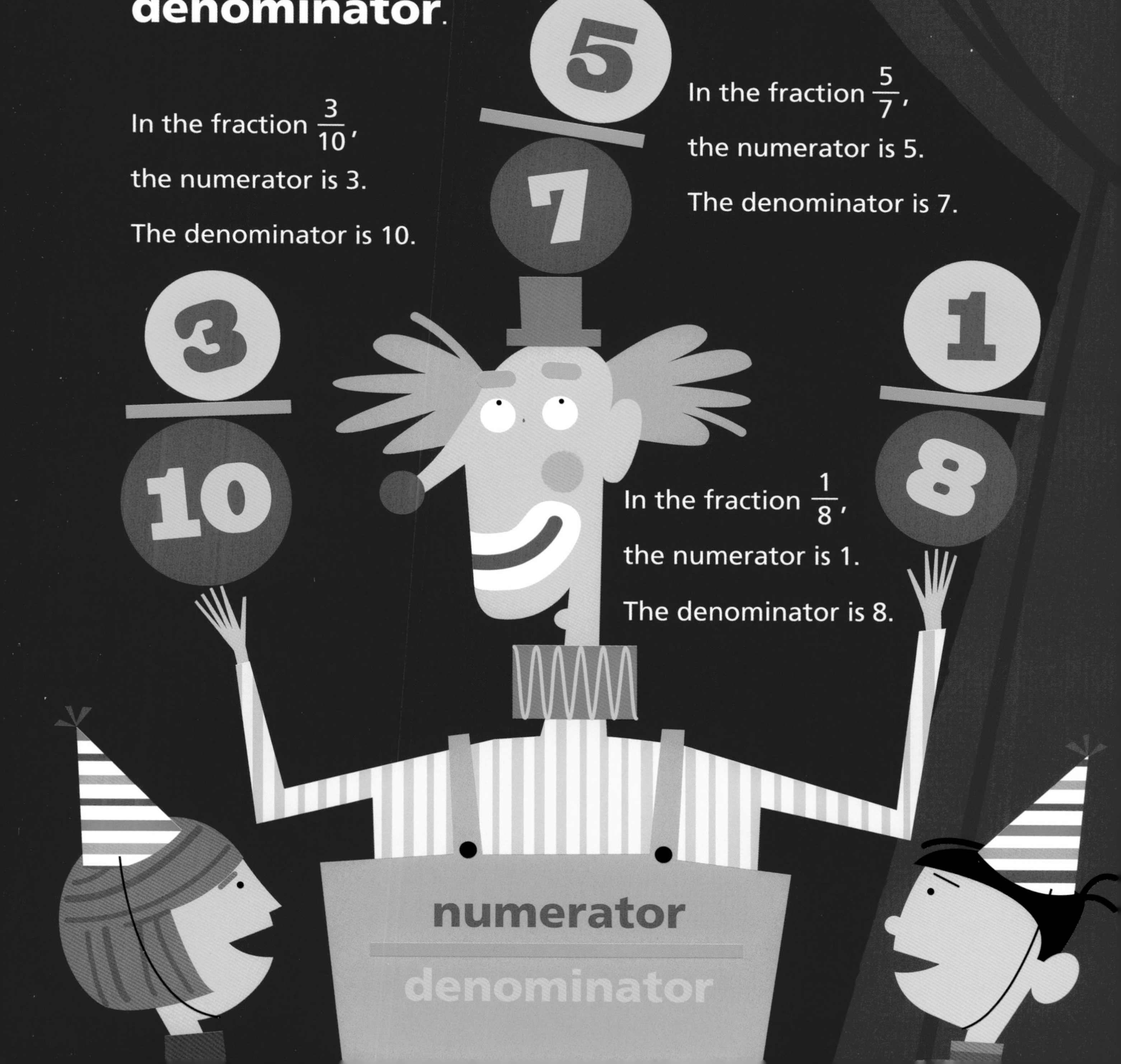

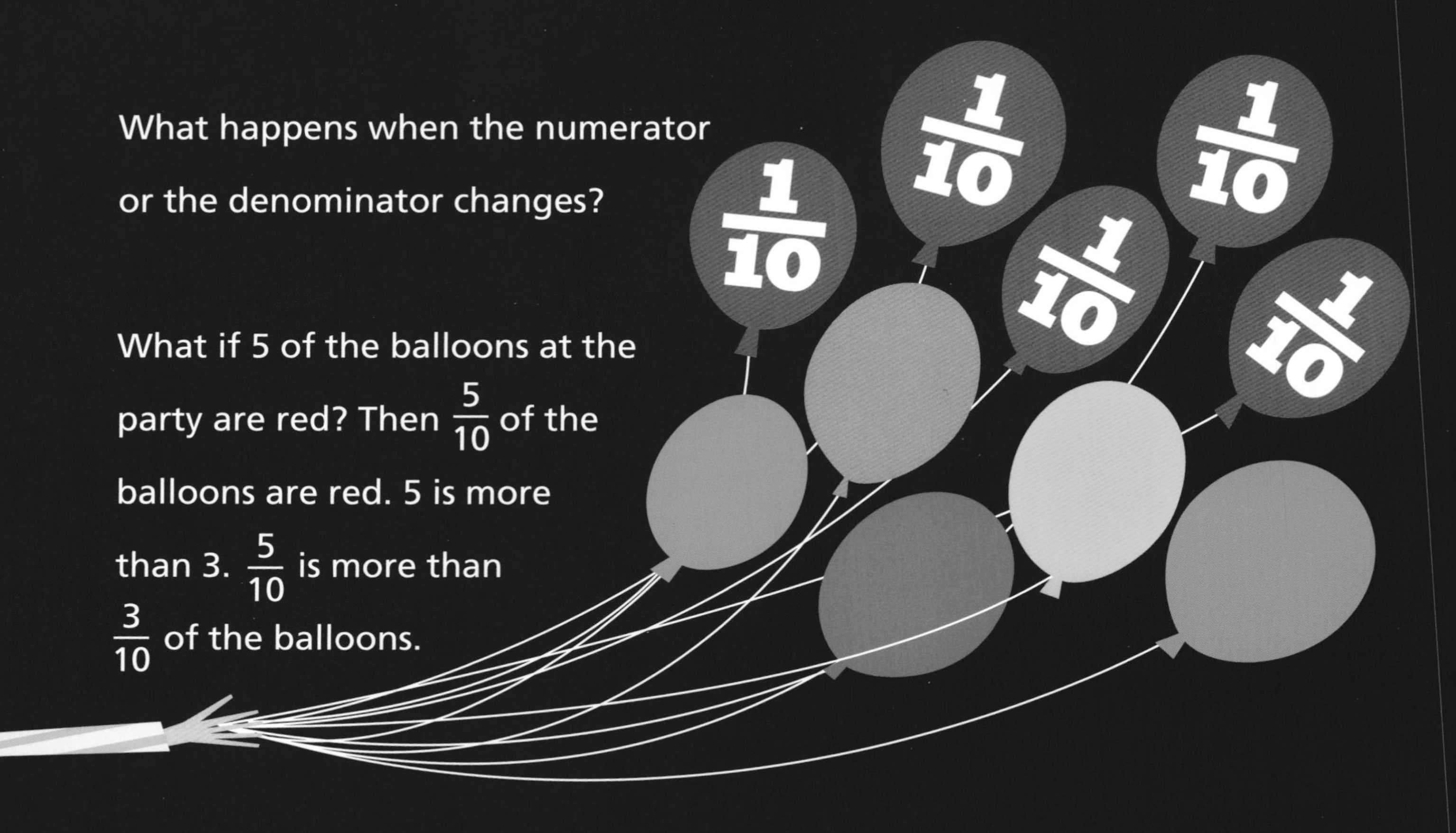

What happens when the numerator or the denominator changes?

What if 5 of the balloons at the party are red? Then $\frac{5}{10}$ of the balloons are red. 5 is more than 3. $\frac{5}{10}$ is more than $\frac{3}{10}$ of the balloons.

What if 6 of the 7 children in the game of musical chairs are sitting? Then $\frac{6}{7}$ of the children are sitting. 6 is more than 5. $\frac{6}{7}$ is more than $\frac{5}{7}$ of the children.

What if you ate 2 slices of pizza?

If you did, you ate $\frac{2}{8}$ of the pizza pie.

2 slices are more than 1 slice.

$\frac{2}{8}$ is more than $\frac{1}{8}$ of the pizza.

The larger the top number of a fraction—the **larger** the **numerator**—the **larger** the **fraction** when the denominators, the bottom numbers, are the same.

At the birthday party, what if the pizza pie was not cut into 8 equal-sized slices? What if it was cut into 10 equal-sized slices? Because more slices were cut from the pie, each slice would be smaller. Each slice would be $\frac{1}{10}$ of the pie. The fraction $\frac{1}{10}$ is smaller than $\frac{1}{8}$ of the same pizza.

At the birthday party, what if the cake was not cut into 12 equal-sized slices? What if it was cut into 15 equal-sized slices? Because more slices were cut from the same cake, each slice would be smaller. Each slice would be $\frac{1}{15}$ of the cake. The fraction $\frac{1}{15}$ is smaller than $\frac{1}{12}$ of the same thing.

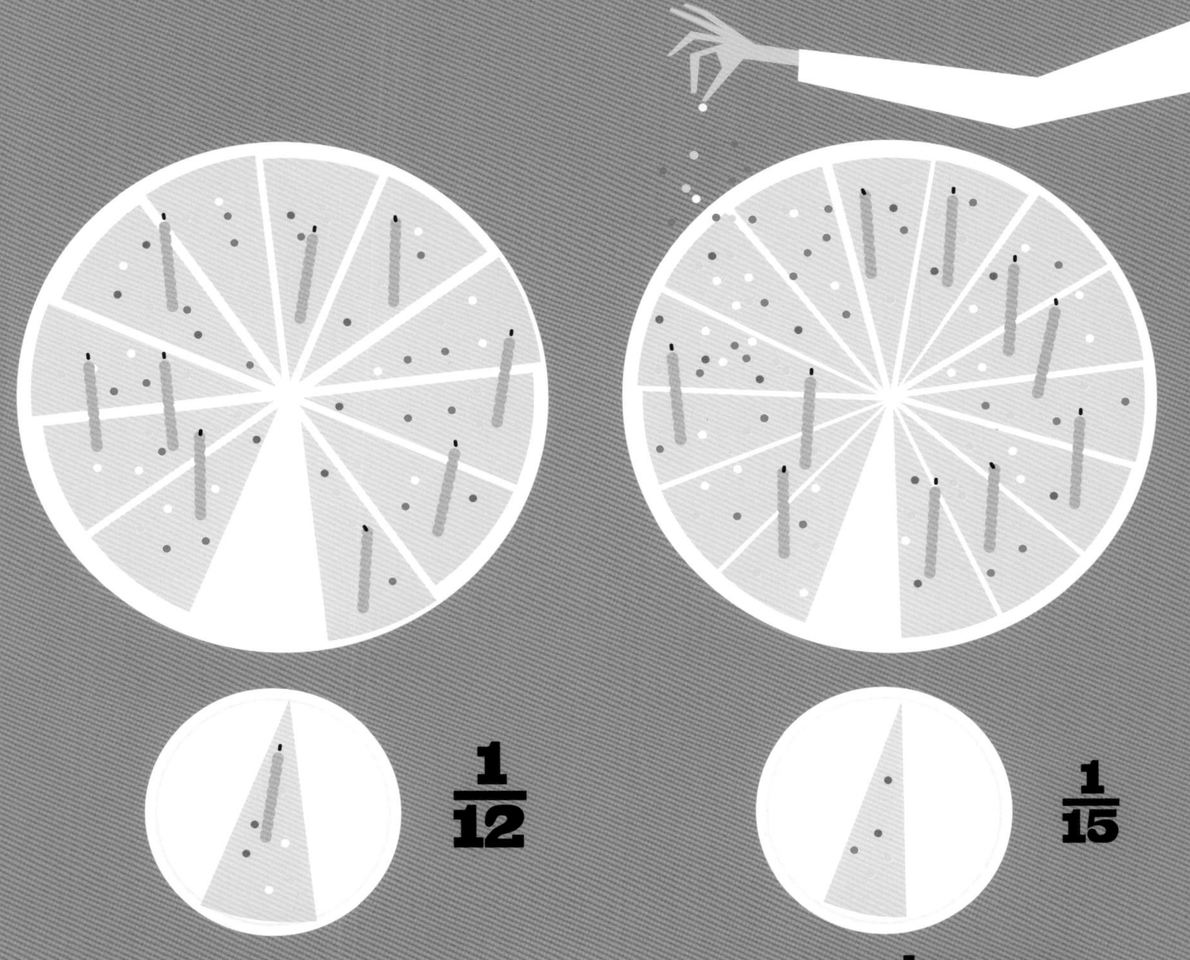

$\frac{1}{12}$ **$\frac{1}{15}$**

The larger the bottom number of a fraction—the **larger** the **denominator**—**the smaller the fraction** when the numerators, the top numbers, are the same.

Folded sheets of paper and crayons can teach you about numerators and denominators.

Here's a sheet of paper that has been carefully folded twice and then unfolded. The 2 creases divide the paper into 4 equal sections. Each section is $\frac{1}{4}$ of the paper.

Take a sheet of paper and fold it so the creases divide the paper into 4 equal sections. Shade 3 sections of the paper red. Shade the remaining section blue.

Take a look at the red and blue sections. The red part, $\frac{3}{4}$ of the paper, is larger than the blue part, $\frac{1}{4}$ of the paper. $\frac{3}{4}$ is more than $\frac{1}{4}$ of the same thing.

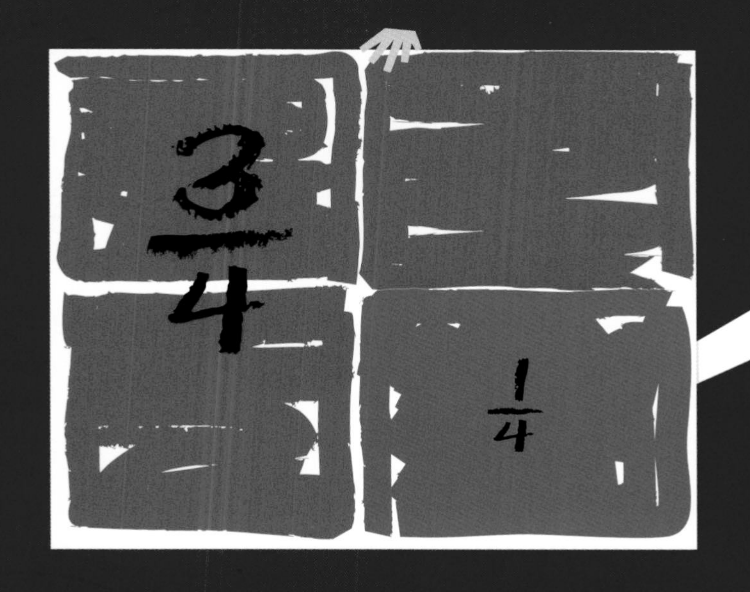

The larger the top number of a fraction—the **larger** the **numerator**—the **larger** the **fraction** when the denominators, the bottom numbers, are the same.

Take another sheet of the same-sized paper and carefully fold it in half. Then unfold it. There's a crease in the middle of the paper. The crease divides the paper into 2 equal sections. Each section is $\frac{1}{2}$ of the paper.

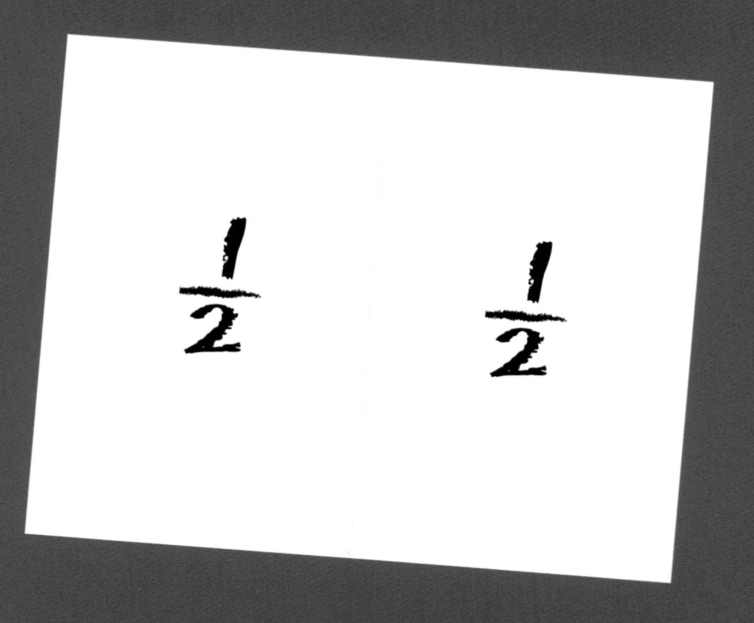

Now shade 1 section, $\frac{1}{2}$, of the paper green.

Next look at the 2 papers. Pay attention to the blue and green sections. The blue section, $\frac{1}{4}$ of the first sheet of paper, is smaller than the green section, $\frac{1}{2}$ of the second sheet of paper. $\frac{1}{4}$ is less than $\frac{1}{2}$ of the same thing.

The larger the bottom number of a fraction—the **larger** the **denominator**—**the smaller the fraction** when the numerators, the top numbers, are the same.

You can play tricks with fractions.

If a birthday cake is cut into equal-sized slices, each slice is the same. But $\frac{1}{12}$ of 1 birthday cake might be more than $\frac{1}{12}$ of another cake. $\frac{1}{12}$ of a large birthday cake is more than $\frac{1}{12}$ of a small cake.

$\frac{1}{12}$ is more than $\frac{1}{15}$ of the same cake.
But $\frac{1}{12}$ of 1 birthday cake might
be less than $\frac{1}{15}$ of another cake.
$\frac{1}{12}$ of a small cake might be less
than $\frac{1}{15}$ of a large cake.

Sometimes the same fraction has different names.

Take 2 white paper plates. Let's pretend each plate is a birthday cake. Before you cut the cake, you decide to serve $\frac{1}{2}$ of it at the party and save $\frac{1}{2}$ of the cake for later.

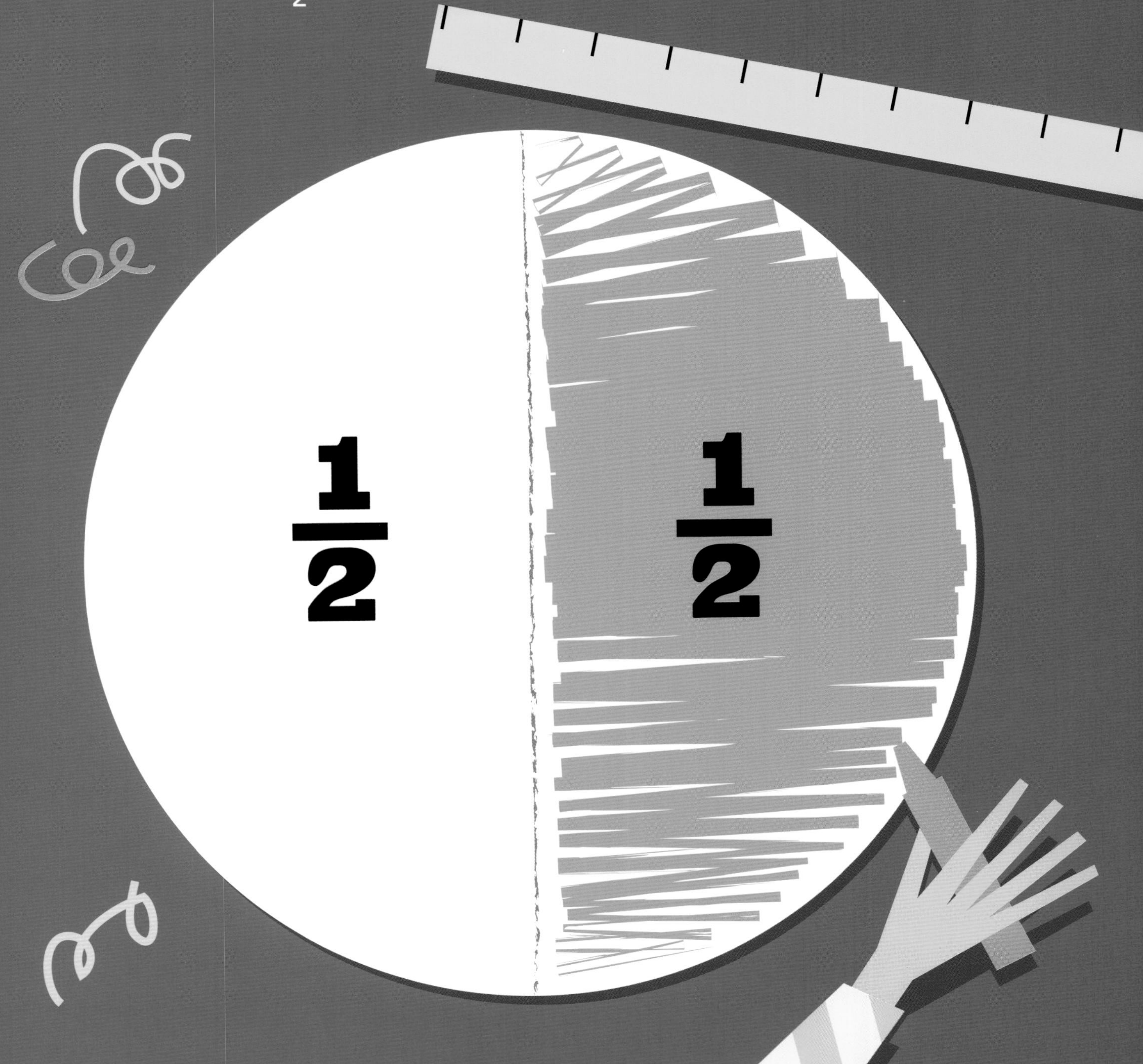

With a ruler and a pencil, draw lines to divide each plate in half. With a crayon, shade $\frac{1}{2}$ of each plate. That's the $\frac{1}{2}$ you will save for later. On 1 plate, divide it again until you have 12 equal-sized pieces.

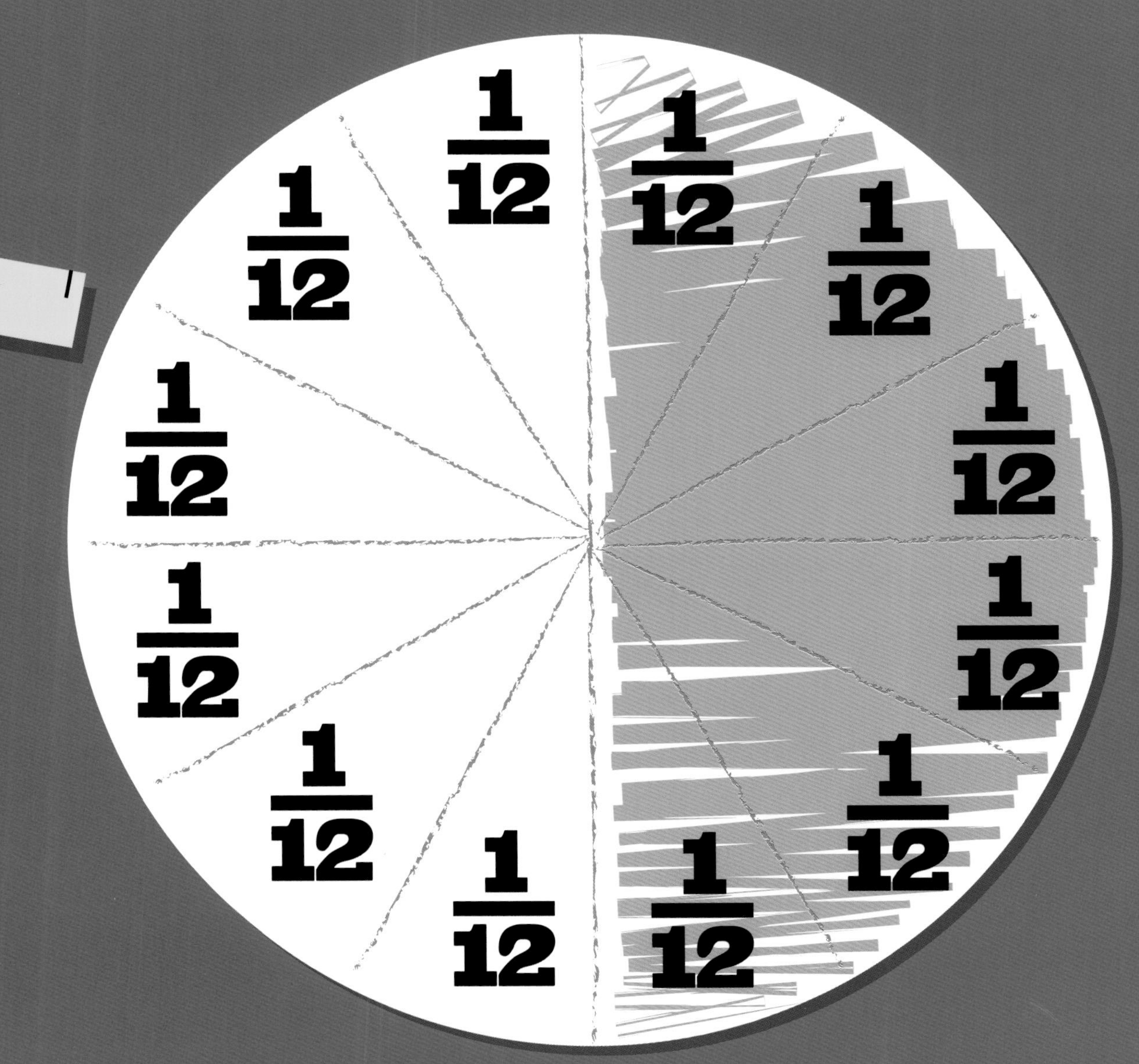

Take a look at the second plate. What was once $\frac{1}{2}$ is now $\frac{6}{12}$. $\frac{1}{2}$ and $\frac{6}{12}$ are really different names for the same fraction. It would be the same if you saved $\frac{1}{2}$ of the cake for later or ate $\frac{6}{12}$ of it.

Now think of pennies and nickels.

5 pennies are $\frac{5}{100}$ of a dollar.

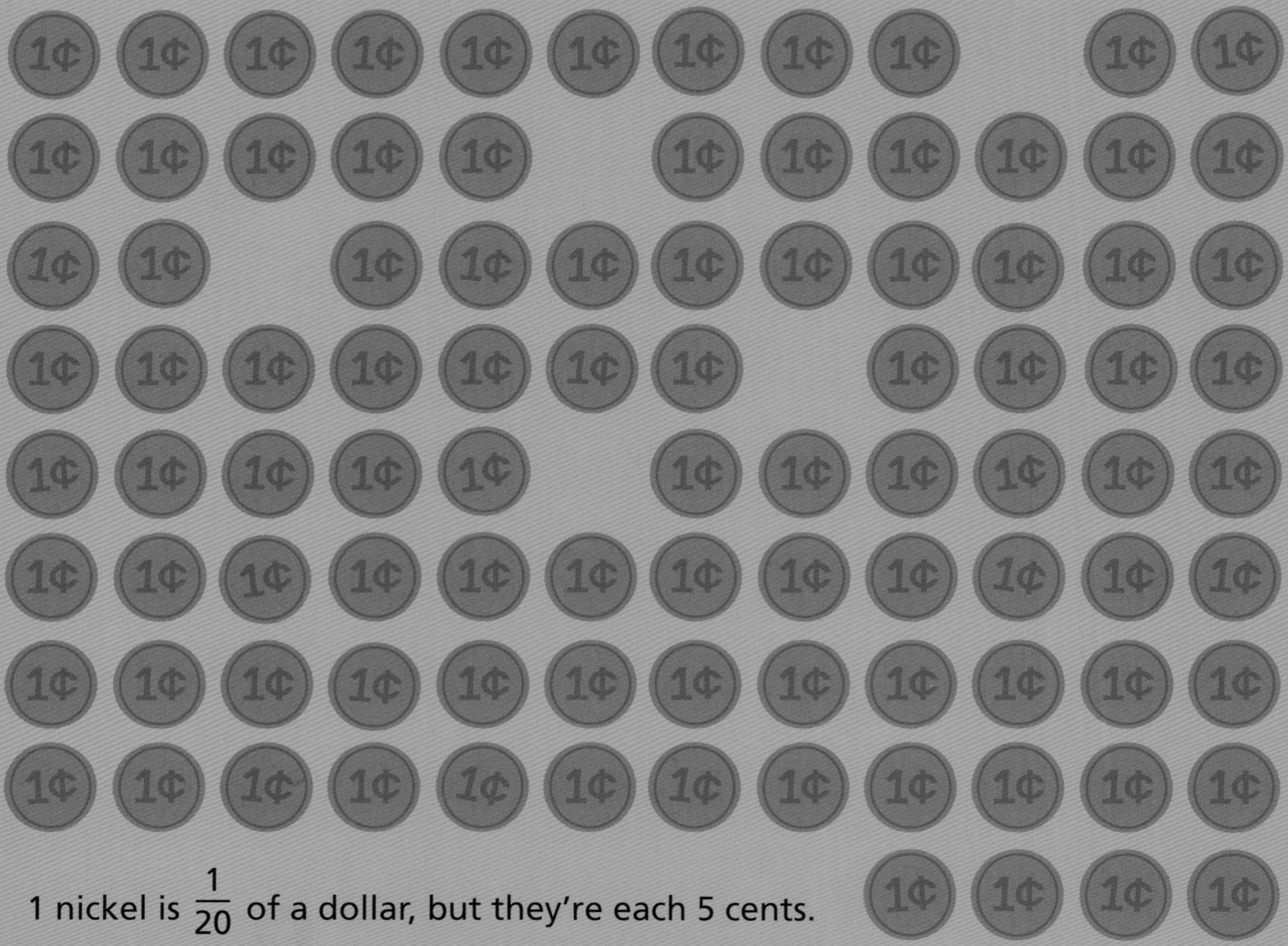

1 nickel is $\frac{1}{20}$ of a dollar, but they're each 5 cents.

$\frac{5}{100}$ is the same as $\frac{1}{20}$.

They are just different names for the same fraction.

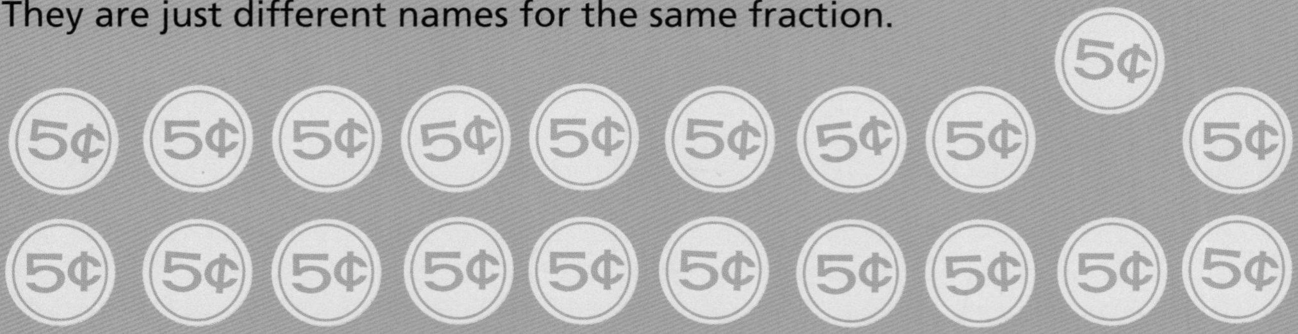

$\frac{8}{8}$ looks like a fraction, but it's really a different name for the number 1.

$\frac{12}{12}$ looks like a fraction, but it's really a different name for the number 1.

Think of a pizza pie that has been cut into 8 slices. Each slice is $\frac{1}{8}$ of the pie. If you ate all 8 slices, $\frac{8}{8}$, you ate 1 whole pie.

Think of that birthday cake that has been cut into 12 slices. Each slice is $\frac{1}{12}$ of the cake. If you ate all 12 slices, you ate $\frac{12}{12}$ of the cake. You ate 1 whole cake.

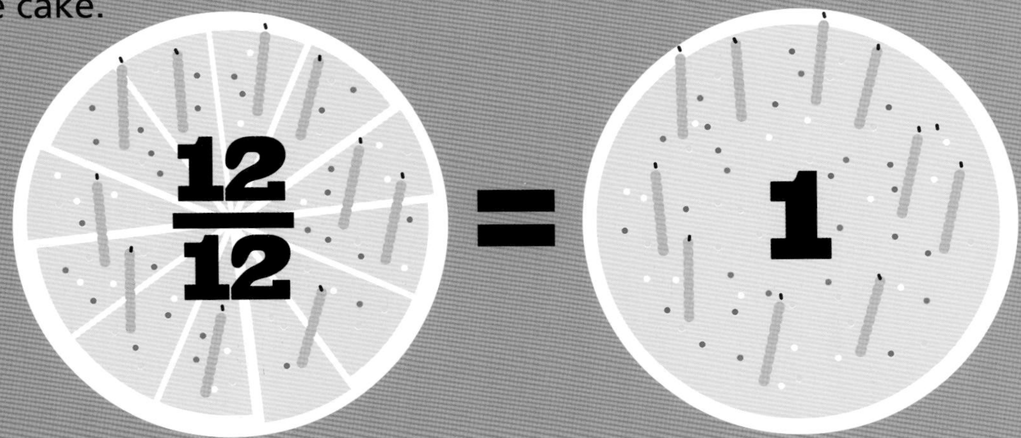

These different names for 1 will help you find different forms of fractions.

What happens when you multiply any number by 1?

The number you start with and your answer are the same.

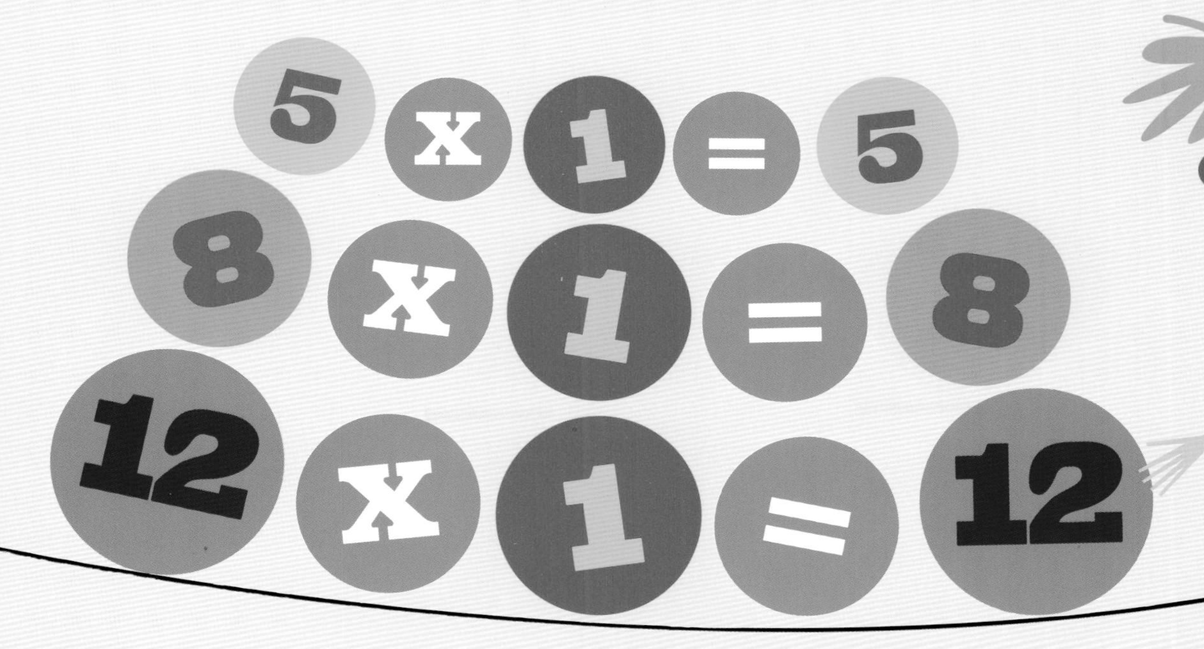

That's also what happens when you multiply fractions by 1.

The fraction you start with and your answer are the same.

$\frac{6}{6}$ is a different form of 1. So,

$\frac{6}{12}$ is another name for $\frac{1}{2}$.

You can find lots of different names for the same fraction. Just multiply the numerator and the denominator by the same number. Just multiply the fraction by 1.

Can you find five different names for $\frac{1}{2}$?

Can you find three different names for $\frac{1}{3}$? For $\frac{2}{3}$?

Think about fractions.

Once you know fractions, you can work with them.

You can add and subtract fractions.

To **add** fractions when the denominators (bottom numbers) are the same, you simply **add** the **numerators** (top numbers) and write your answer over the denominator.

At the birthday party, if you ate 1 slice of pizza, you ate $\frac{1}{8}$ of the pie. If you ate a second slice, you ate $\frac{1}{8}$ more of the pie. You ate $\frac{2}{8}$ of the pie.

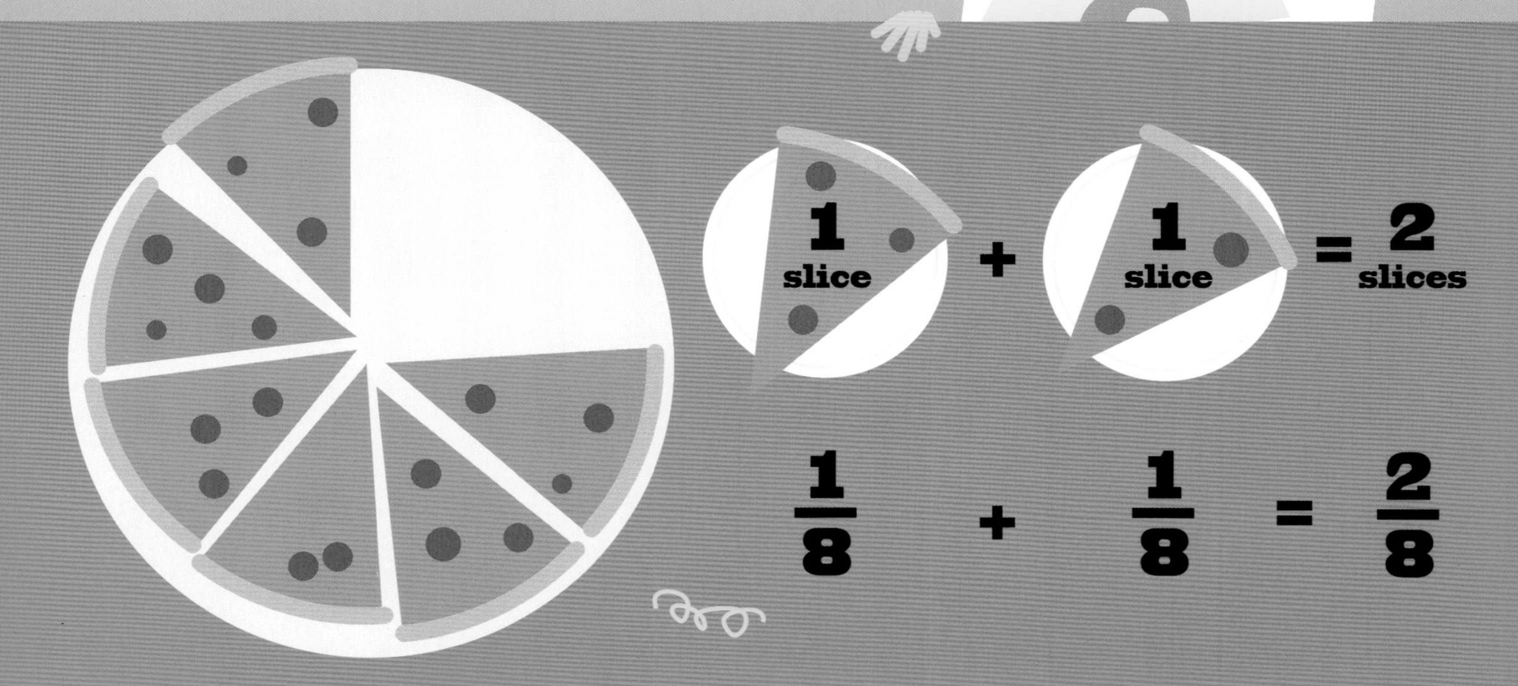

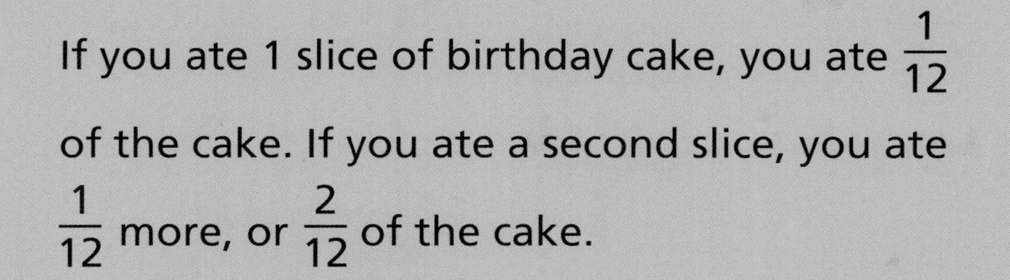

If you ate 1 slice of birthday cake, you ate $\frac{1}{12}$ of the cake. If you ate a second slice, you ate $\frac{1}{12}$ more, or $\frac{2}{12}$ of the cake.

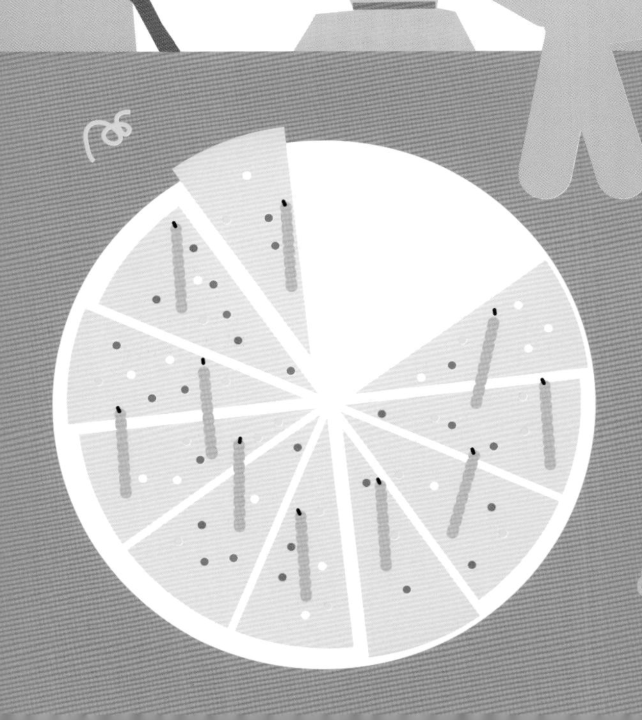

1 slice + 1 slice = 2 slices

$$\frac{1}{12} + \frac{1}{12} = \frac{2}{12}$$

To **subtract** fractions when the denominators are the same, you simply **subtract** the **numerators** and write your answer over the denominator.

At the birthday party, if you asked for 3 slices of pizza, you asked for $\frac{3}{8}$ of the pie. If you ate just 2 slices, you ate $\frac{2}{8}$ of the pie. You would have 1 slice left.

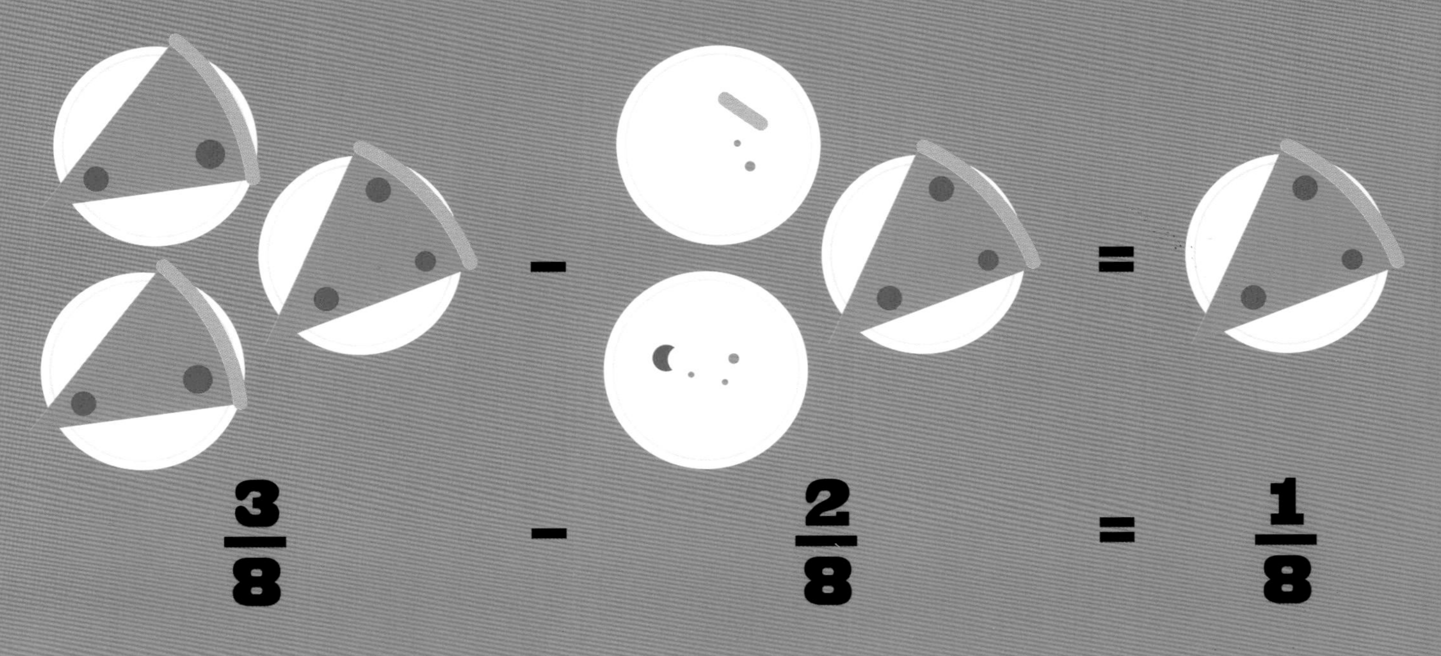

$$\frac{3}{8} - \frac{2}{8} = \frac{1}{8}$$

At the party, if you asked for 2 slices of birthday cake, you asked for $\frac{2}{12}$ of the cake. If you ate just 1 slice, you ate $\frac{1}{12}$ of the cake.

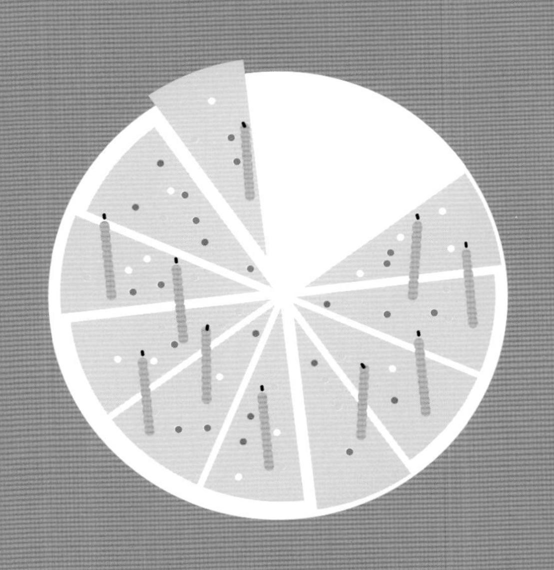

$$\frac{2}{12} - \frac{1}{12} = \frac{1}{12}$$

Fractions are at birthday parties.

Fractions are at football games.

Fractions are in shoe stores.

Fractions are in clothing stores.

People use fractions to tell time.

People often use fractions.

Fractions are everywhere.

The time is $\frac{1}{4}$ past 6 o'clock.

For Uncle Ben,
congratulations
on your special
birthday
—D. A. A.

For John Grandits,
who taught me the
ins and outs of
bookmaking
—E. M.

Printed and Bound in April 2011 at Tien Wah Press,
Johor Bahru, Johor, Malaysia.
www.holidayhouse.com
3 5 7 9 10 8 6 4

Library of Congress Cataloging-in-Publication Data

Adler, David A.
Working with fractions / by David A. Adler ;
illustrated by Edward Miller III.
— 1st ed.
p. cm.
ISBN-13: 978-0-8234-2010-0
ISBN-10: 0-8234-2010-8
1. Fractions—Juvenile literature.
I. Miller, Edward, 1964- ill. II. Title.
QA117.A256 2007
513.2'6—dc22
2006049687

ISBN 978-0-8234-2207-4 (paperback)

The art for this book was created on a computer.
The fonts used in this book are Frutiger,
Blackoak, and Egbert.
Book design by Edward Miller.

The author
and artist thank
Professor Stephen Krulik
of the Department of
Curriculum, Instruction,
and Technology in
Education of Temple
University for
his help.